THE LONG WAY DOWN

A Sequence of Poems of Grief and Hope

THE
LONG

WAY

DOWN

A Sequence of Poems of Grief and Hope

Averil Stedeford

IN MEMORY OF BRIAN

With grateful thanks to Elizabeth and Kevin for their
support, encouragement and gentle editing.

By the same author

FACING DEATH, *Patients, Families and Professionals*
1984 and 1994 (Second Edition)

Ellipse and Other Poems, 1990

The Long Way Down
Averil Stedeford

Published, printed and bound by Aspect Design
89 Newtown Road, Malvern, Worcs. WR14 1PD United Kingdom
Tel: 01684 561567 E-mail: allan@aspect-design.net
Website: www.aspect-design.net

Part one

THE LONG WAY DOWN

Part two

GRIEF AND HOPE

Part three

HOSPICE POEMS

THE LONG WAY DOWN

The sun was bright, the sea was blue,
it felt like holiday. We climbed the cliff path,
spread our picnic at the top,
close to the steep drop past jagged rocks
down to the beating sea.

I offered him some cake. He wasn't there.
Only days before, we learned the news:
"For this cancer, nothing can be done."

Gripped by fear, I could not look down.
Above the noise of gulls I heard a call
found him clinging to the coastguard rail
where he had run to foil the urge to jump.

Holding close, we faced what might have been
and what we knew would come,
re-pledged our love,
thankful that he chose the long way down.

SHOES ON
(Written when red tape and bureaucracy got the better of us)

I need to go out.
Please help me put my shoes on.
> *The shoe finder will come in about an hour.*

Only one shoe?
> *Right foot person puts right shoes on.*
> *Doesn't do left feet.*

What about you?
> *Not trained.*
> *Left foot person has had a baby.*
> *Back in eight weeks.*

Go barefoot?
> *Right foot shoe remover not free until tomorrow.*
> *Barefoot not allowed.*

Wear sandals?
> *Sandal shop has closed down.*
> *Purchase of sandals must be put out to tender.*

Cut off feet?
> *No chopper.*

SPARROW

Fear not; you are worth more than any number of sparrows.

Matthew 10, v 31

You are my sparrow.
Yes, there are lots more
but you are mine.
I have been watching you,
know you are afraid.

Come and let me hold you
smooth your wings
feel your racing heart.

I have made a hollow of my palm.
Settle in and rest.
My other hand will cover you,
fingers parted so you can look out
until you feel so safe
you fall asleep.

Then I will keep you,
wait until I feel you stir and stretch,
open out my hands,
watch you fly.

BARBER

In hospital I trimmed your scraggy beard
which garnished all our kisses
gathered biscuit crumbs
and frightened little children.

Back home I shook the towel on the grass.
Balls of wiry hair rolled in the wind,
began to blow away. I ran about

gathering all I could
to tuck into the compost,
you in the garden
for ever.

LOOKING THROUGH

A week before
I found him lying, staring at the ceiling.
Studying a spider?

"I am looking **through** the ceiling"
he said, in such a tone
I felt chastised
yet drawn to stay and watch
his arms unfold
shoulders loosen, sink into the bed.

A smile began, opening his lips.
It smoothed his brow, lit his eyes
shone through his wasted face.
I crept away
wondering.

DYING

By invasion
    explosion
    seizing up
    wearing thin
dying breaks the body
frees the soul.

Suddenly or slowly
with struggle or ease
the door opens.

Part two

GRIEF AND HOPE

NOW

I write with his pen
drink from his mug
use up his Ovaltine
and sleep in the room
where I counted breaths
watched the throes
held his cooling hand.

BAMBOO COFFIN

First thought – a picnic hamper
then a Moses basket.
More like a coracle
robust enough for sailing home.

As I threaded raffia through its weave
to tie tomorrow's flowers
I looked inside, saw the sturdy frame
and thought 'I'd feel safe in here'.

Everyone brought something to the church:
a rosebud, dahlia, tiny cyclamen
lemon balm and rosemary
conkers hung on strings, autumn leaves.

Soon all the ties were used. To thread some more
I pushed a long curved needle through the weft
just above his nose, his knees, his feet.
At the time it seemed quite natural.

Through the crowded nave the coffin went.
Conkers bumped like fenders.
My rose stood tall above the blaze of flowers.
A red leaf fell.

The congregation sang of faith and grief.
Committal prayers were said; the coffin launched.
Its ashes rest with his in a favourite wood;
its smoke has risen with him.

The comparison of the coffin with a coracle was particularly
apt as the church where the funeral took place was dedicated
to Saint Columba who crossed from Ireland in a coracle to
bring Christianity to Iona and beyond.

SHADOW

At the funeral
they all said what a happy man he was.
Even a happy man has a shadow.
His stayed at home
fell on all of us.

ONE LOO ROLL

lasts so long now you have gone.
Just like grief
it goes on and on.

GONE-NESS

I cannot say you **have** gone
as if you might come back.
You used to be in one place at a time.
Mostly I knew where.

Now I say you **are** gone.
Your absence walks with me.
So many empty spaces wear your shape.
Your gone-ness everywhere.

TODAY

Love pads out the sharpest edge of grief
blunting stabs to blows
which bruise but cannot kill.
Today I wish they could.

CLEANING THE ROOM

When we knew it must be single beds
I cleaned the spare room
moved the furniture
hung his favourite pictures
made space to hide his dressings.

His surprise and pleasure was a joy,
easing my weariness.
He only wanted one more change,
the mirror,
not to be confronted by his face.

I almost lived there
eating, sewing, listening to music,
carrying, emptying, washing.
He always smiled as I undressed for bed
  each night a touching moment
  his own strip-tease.

That was where he died
and I prayed over him,
escaped into the garden
when the white van came.

Now I clean again,
wash off small splashes.
I leave the pictures, put the mirror back.
Dressing gown to OXFAM, bin the slippers
listen to a requiem as I shine the windows
make the room my own.

LONELY

My ears are lonely for the little sounds of you.
My hair is lonely for an unpaid touch.
My hands are lonely; feel forever gloved.
My breasts are lonely. A bra gives no caress.
Only the NHS observes my nakedness.

PATCHWORK

Wartime blackout, scraps from family sewing
even curtain fabrics found a place
as patches to be joined by hand to make
a spread of memories for our double bed.

Progress was slow. I stowed it in the loft.
Years later I was pleased to see the colours
were still bright, the patterns full of life.
And it would almost fit a single bed.

I took it up again
sewing while I kept him company.
"Not until I'm gone!" he said, and laughed
hearing how I planned to finish it.

Now I have a coverlet
edged with patches from his favourite shirts
ties that tell his story
his nearly new pyjamas.

APPLE

Too frail to go to Harvest Festival
he made it down our garden in his chair,
picked all the apples from his little Cox
a full lap.

At Christmas I unwrapped the first,
mouthed its cold skin hungrily.
Just apple.

After grief, sweet crispness
a little sacrament.

THE FORTY-NINTH VALENTINE

We always exchanged Valentines
tender, funny, sexy
never too expensive.

This year I'm going to buy
the dearest one he'd like,
address:
'c/o St Peter,
Heavenly Mansions'
And post it. Airmail?

What will the sorter do?
No sender to return it to.
Not like the letters sent to Santa Claus
for which there is a protocol.

Perhaps an office girl will tear hers up
send mine to her love;
enjoy the sweetest kiss she's ever had.

MRS CLOCK

He loved repairing clocks.
She became receptionist
explaining why some jobs took extra time,
finder of lost screws, admirer of skilled work
consoler when he cracked a precious dial
proof-reader for his writing
first-aider when his hand was slashed
by an escaping spring.

Turret Clock events were always fun:
treasure hunts to churches and town halls
where dusty steps led up to hefty works,
some smithy-made, cramped below the bells.
Museums, stately homes were scanned for clocks.
She looked at marquetry and painted dials
rubicund moon-faces, rocking ships
while he was occupied with gears and wheels.

Now he is dead and Mrs. Clock dies with him.
The workshop too. No tick, no chime or strike,
his head-lamp curves round nothing.
Only the smells remain: solvents, polish, oils,
Unused his tools and books, lathes and battered bench.

She scrubs the workshop floor and locks the door.
In the house she winds two favourite clocks,
a seventeenth century lantern
and one from a signal box.

OPPORTUNITY

This death I grieve so much
provides God an opportunity
to move into the centre of my life:
take up the empty space within
greet me every morning
sleep with me at night.

I need not forsake
what is good,
or nudge out anyone.
God does not ask
to be alone with me,
Just number one.

AMBIVALENCE

I *don't* want to wear your socks
but my toes are cold and they fit.
They even look nice with my trousers
but they should be on *your* feet.

I must want to wear your socks
since I have put them on.
They didn't go in the charity bag
to keep another man warm.

So I do want to wear your socks?
The answer is *Yes and No*
just like I wanted to keep you
and wanted to let you go.

FACECLOTH

Packing my bag for the first holiday
I picked out the flannel that washed him last.

At bed time, amazement. A sweet tongued kiss.
How could a cloth convey love, and like this?
Where it was placed I leave you to guess.

I thought of the woman who touched Christ's robe,
of healing relics, the Turin shroud.
I never expected to join that crowd.

SEEING LEAVES

Last year when you were ill
Meg and I walked through the park alone.
She sniffed and waited while I picked up leaves
red and yellow, silver backed and brown.

Back home I set them out on your tray
a chestnut's fan of leaflets: curvy oak
pointed maple, golden flakes of birch.
You looked at them, fingered them

as if you'd never seen such leaves before
as if your hands and eyes were taking you
walking through the trees where we had been,
perhaps beyond.

This year the leaves were just as colourful.
I shuffled through them like a little child
enjoying them until I picked one up
and remembered.

I took some to a friend who is blind.
"Each kind's a different size!" he said
amazed as an astronomer
discovering a new star.

He felt how oak leaves curve, maples point,
read their skin like Braille,
traced the veins joining to meet the stem
wanted to know their names

and colours too. What brown or red
conjured in his mind he could not say
but his delight at their variety
shone through all his face, except his eyes.

Each year since then
Autumn brings two men
to enhance its grace, one blind, one dead.

SECOND CHRISTMAS

I put up the lights as you did
the holly wreath on the door
I potted the tree as you did.
This year it hurts more.

I've no one to complain at
for crooked candle-lights
no reason now to buy the box
of dates you specially liked.

Please squeeze down the chimney
if only for awhile.
Be real as Father Christmas
to a little child.

Come down and leave a blessing,
I won't mind the soot.
If you will give me just one kiss
I'll smile as a grandma should
and grow up.

A SURPRISE?

Clearing out his desk, I found
a book of Shakespeare's sonnets
small, gold tooled, red-bound
with no inscription.
'Brand new,' I thought.
'Perhaps a gift for me,
brought home from a trip,
long forgotten.' But

there were three places marked
with pressed forget-me-nots.
'Sweet love,' the first began.
The next 'I must confess
that we two must be twain.'
The last 'No more be grieved
at that which thou hast done.'

Shock. Then angry tears.
Not difficult to guess
who marked those passages.
Grief gave way to pity.
He never did read verse.

EXACTLY RIGHT

Sometimes I talked to him.
"It's nearly two years on.
My heart still aches.
By now I really know
that you have gone
into eternity, forever."

"That's exactly right." he said
sitting on the bottom of my bed.
We laughed out loud at this absurdity.
Then he was gone.
No chance to ask him anything.

MRS CLOCK AGAIN

The railway clock was given to a grandson.
My brother has our father's grandfather.
The lantern and Scottish regulator
were lodgers with a friend while I moved house.

For a year I had to do without them.
Protected from the builders' dust, they waited.
Delivered, they were welcomed like old friends
who tick and strike, make my house a home.
I hugged the tall one and began to weep,
        unaware I was expecting him
                to accompany them.

Two years on, his customers still ring.
I explain, hear my words fall heavily
        as I say goodbye.

DOUBLE DELIGHT

        is not the name of a new ice cream.
        After all these years of grief
        I am
                enjoying
                enjoying
                        myself.

AFTERMATH

Grass growing after mowing or harvest

Look at my field!
Each day it's growing greener.

When the Reaper took you
he left stubble, only fit for burning.
No refuge, even for a rabbit.

Dry grief turned to tears.

Now ideas sprout, projects flower.
Your death has set me free
to grow a different crop.

It is unspeakable
but the green blades whisper
"I'm almost glad you died."

Is this bright sky
dancing in the puddles
your reply?

A SHOUT

The cobbled street was narrow
a tight fit for a hearse.
As they eased the coffin in
a priest we knew approached.
He stopped to cross himself
then rode away.

I longed to call his name,
break from the crowd,
cry out to him
"It's Brian! my Brian"

I wanted to see the shock
watch his fine face change
as he dismounted,
hear what he would say of consolation.

But I am English.
I kept quiet. Four years on
I still wish I'd shouted
so I'm doing it now.

Part three

HOSPICE POEMS

POEMS WRITTEN WHILE WORKING AT
SIR MICHAEL SOBELL HOUSE, OXFORD

THE LAST INVITATION

The tide was out as two children played
through a hot summer day by the sea,
building their castles with ramparts and flags
where later the water would be.

The sea crept in as they finished their work.
The waves as they came seemed to say
to one "We will ruin the castle you've made."
To the other they said "Come and play."

The first built a wall as high as he could
to keep his proud fortress from harm.
"Go back" he yelled at the charging waves
and he jumped from their surge in alarm.

Relentless, the sea swept over the wall
and flattened the work of his spade.
His castle was gone and he trudged slowly home
angry and sad and dismayed.

"It's coming" the other said. "Quickly I'll dig
a gully to channel the sea
and a moat so the water can rush all around
to make it an island for me."

He stood on his towers, not minding their fall
as the water came rippling round.
When a great wave washed right over it all
he laughed as he leapt to dry ground.

The tide will come in for you and me
as it did for those children that day.
Does it only destroy? Dare we believe
it's a last invitation to play?

IF WHEELCHAIR WERE A PRAM

In wheels I sit
and steer myself around,
thinking it was in wheels
I travelled first down bumpy paths
to lie beneath the trees and sleep,
or wonder at the movement of the leaves.

Pram-bound explorers' feet have never felt
the ground their wheels compress.
I wish paralysis brought with it innocence.
I weep because I know what lies beyond the fence
where dead legs will not go.

If wheelchair were a pram then I could throw
a toy or rattle crashing to the ground
to ease my rage. I would know,
but they would laugh, not blame,
thinking it was just a baby's game.

Babies cannot speak as I can.
Nor can they recall Christmases or courting.
Is speech a gain when every word is sad?
Memory increases grief for me.
Return me to my pram.

NEW WHEELS

A very private man, he came through grief
when someone dared to spring the trap of solitude,
a trundling cart, rattling him to early execution.

New wheels he bought, ingeniously controlled,
a wheelchair so responsive to his touch
that it could take him almost anywhere.

The greying engineer took much delight
in this invention; new technology
as canny as himself. Down the street he rode
over the curb and into the village shop
to buy his baccy, wink at girls,
and talk about the cricket.

For six good weeks he travelled cheerfully,
grumbled a bit, but was a man again.
His last wheels were the hearse
that took him down the old familiar street.
The curse of death had lifted weeks before.
Only his useless body went through the chapel door.

FAMILIARITY

Why is John so scared?
He can't rest on his pillow.
We thought he would be happier
if we moved him near the window.

He spent half the war in a prison cell
each crack, each crevice in the walls
he knew them all so well.
"In here I keep remembering.
when they rescued me.
Our fellows had to **pull me** out.
They called it 'setting free.'"

He sank into his pillows
as they trundled back his bed.
He didn't trust their kindly words
for fear they hid contempt
but when he reached his usual place
his smile was eloquent.

THE RED HAT

"You must not grieve for me," her husband said.
"You know how it upsets me if you cry.
Be cheerful at my funeral.
Wear my favourite dress, your bright red hat."

For months she wondered why she felt so ill:
half alive and useless. "I'm not sad"
she said to her G.P. He read her face
and sent her on to me.

I listened, found a pen, began to draw
two circles. These are you and John
when you first met. Life and love
moulded you to fit against each other.

Now you are left in very painful shape.
Everywhere he used to touch is raw.
It will hurt, becoming round again.

Your tears will be like water
a potter throws on clay
to ease the changing form.

Let yourself remember.
Go home now and grieve.

And she did.

THE BEAST

'How well you look' they say. But I am ill, and know it.
'You're brown. Your holiday has done you good.'
They chat and go their way, but I am ill, and know it.
The weakness gnaws. Strange pain I cannot place
threatens and frightens me.

'All normal' says the doctor. 'X-rays, tests
show there is nothing wrong.' It must be nerves.
With 'You'll be better soon' he nods and smiles
and hands a script for pills. He understands.
His tranquiliser serves to stir my rage.
Its implication bids me disengage
so I retreat, for I am ill and know it.

But do I know? The doctor might be right.
Perhaps I'm being haunted by a ghost,
a shadow beast, dissolving at first light.
No! This beast bites. It whines that I am ill
both day and night.

This could be madness. Just imagining.
Can everyone be blind to what is happening?
Their sideways looks and cardboard sympathy,
the subtle doubts that strip my friends from me
clothe me in shame. I wait, at home, alone
until the insistent ringing of the phone
heralds an answer.

At last they've named the illness, caught the beast!
This news that is both sentence and release
sinks slowly in. Now all the shame
woven of disbelief, can fall away
as one by one folk come, recovering me.

Redressed by love, I grieve that I will die.
Yet as I weep, a quick surprising joy
comes racing in, strong and enlivening.
I learn, as friends renew their faith in me
death matters less than my integrity.

THE PRIEST

He would not lie in his fresh-smoothed bed
where fiends had plagued him through the night
so he slumped beside it, waiting.
Although a priest, the gift of peace
was not for him when dying.

Chin down, lids shut, and thick neck bent,
exhausted from his wrestling,
only the twitching of his frown
revealed he was still dreaming.

I tried to wake him for I guessed
his visions were as gripping
as any horror film, but he
was totally withdrawn from me
wrapped up in them, and suffering.

Desperate, I saw a cup of tea
left on his locker, cooling.
"Would you like a drink?" I said,
not for a moment thinking
that he would speak, But
when a man is fraught like this
anything's worth trying.

No answer, so I took his hand
and wrapped it round the cup,
wondering if, where words had failed
some act might wake him up.

Slowly we raised it to his lips
until the warm tea touched them.
He took a few labourious sips
then stopped. His eyes were open.
He had changed. Somehow I knew
that words could now be spoken.

"Over the years you've given a cup
to many." This he heard.
Eyes met and so did we.
A sacrament of lukewarm tea
had brought us to a crossing.
His agony, like Calvary
gave way at last to yielding.
We eased him gently into bed
to deep and tranquil sleeping.

DYING TWICE

Death once dead, there's no more dying then.
Shakespeare   Sonnet 146

The bard seems sure, but I think he forgot
Lazarus, who staggered from his tomb
summoned by his friend's almighty shout
"Lazarus, come out!"
He must have died again.

Now, when some folk die, their inert hearts
can be restarted by a well placed shock.
Of those, a few describe
floating above their bed,
watching the resuscitation team
till they were jolted back and found themselves
looking up at faces looking down
anxious and relieved.

Others recall how they were led
through darkness to a bright appealing light,
or glided through a tunnel, quite at ease,
behind a guide they almost recognized.
Eager to go on, they felt recalled
to finish something they had left half-done,
or heard an urgent voice; perhaps a child,
not to be orphaned yet.

All the revived die twice.
We are not told what Lazarus made of this
but we can learn from our contemporaries.
For some, anxiety ruins extra time.
They dare not play lest they risk death again.
But others know a deep, contented peace.
Their fear has gone.
Each day is a new coin to be spent
on small delights they would, by rights, have missed.
They say to those of us who dread the end:
It may be safer, easier than you think.
When Death met me I thought he was a friend.

THE HEAVY STONE

My grief was a heavy stone, rough and sharp.
Grasping to pick it up my hands were cut.
Afraid to let it go I carried it.
While I had my grief you were not lost.

The rain of my tears smoothed it.
The wind of my rage weathered it,
making it round and small.

The cuts in my hands have healed.
Now in my palm it rests,
sometimes almost beautiful,
sometimes almost you.

NOTES ON THE HOSPICE POEMS

Most of these poems appeared in print in the second edition of my book FACING DEATH Patients Families and Professionals. Heinemann, the first publisher, told me poetry did not belong in medical books and forced me to turn them into prose.

The last invitation.

This poem was a favourite of Viv Pritchard, the 'matron'. She used it when she talked to children in schools about the work of a hospice.

The 'wheel chair poems'

The man at the centre of these two poems had been profoundly depressed for a very long time. His GP wrote that he and his wife had a very difficult relationship. I used these poems to teach that depression should always be treated in terminal illness. It is not a normal component of the dying process. I asked his GP to increase his antidepressant and did some work with the couple, to which they were responsive despite their long unhappy history. The practice helped him to obtain the wheelchair which made such a difference. He died at home, and was only bedfast for the last week. I showed these poems to his widow at follow up and she exclaimed "You've got him!"

Familiarity

I had several patients with inexplicable distress from whom I elicited a history of dreadful wartime experiences. For them death had seemed inevitable. It is as if the psyche asks itself "When did I last feel like this?" and the terrible memories come flooding back. Once this is recognised they are repressed again and the patient can relax in the knowledge that they will die well cared for, in a comfortable bed.

The red hat

Suppressed grief often expresses itself as physical symptoms which do not respond to treatment. If they do, a new symptom soon appears. I explained to this patient that it was her husband's love for her that made him ask her not to grieve. He did not understand how important it was for her to do so. The GP reported that this intervention was successful.

The beast

This poem draws on the experience of suffering for long time with an undiagnosed illness as often happens with cancer of the pancreas. I used this poem in teaching GPs and I could see from their attentive faces that this was familiar and perplexing territory. One later told me The Beast haunted him every time he could find nothing wrong with a perpetually complaining patient.

Once I was asked to prepare a court report for two sisters who were suing the GP who had cared for their late father. He had been ill and steadily getting worse over a period of two years. For each complaint he was given a pain killer, cough linctus, or some non-specific remedy, and no investigations had been done. Eventually one of his daughters took him to her own doctor who sent him into hospital. Five days later he died of widespread cancer.

I wrote my report as expert witness and on impulse added this poem, not a usual step to take! In due course I was called to a meeting with solicitors and the Queen's Council. There I learned that the poem had been tremendously helpful in preparing the case. The patient's father had written letters to his daughters during his illness, and prompted by the poem they re-read them, discovering that what their father described of his suffering tallied closely with my account in The Beast. They felt truly understood, and justified in their action. Counsel thought the poem was very powerful and planned to use it in court. "It would impress the judge" she said. I was secretly disappointed that the matter was settled out of court. Never-the-less the poem had done a good job.

The priest

This poem needs no explanation other than the fact that this man was suffering from kidney failure, the biochemical changes of which are difficult to treat in terminal illness. I can only think that somehow the act which we shared reactivated his sense of his priesthood and brought with it peace.

The heavy stone

This poem has been used a lot by bereavement counselors with their clients, including children. They bring with them to the first session a selection of stones and invite the client to choose one which best represents where they are in their grief. This helps them to talk and gives an expectation of progress. They are given a copy of the poem nicely printed out on a card as a keepsake at the last session.

Index of first lines